A U T H O R ' S   N O T E

One of the ways that animals communicate
is by the noises they make. The noises can signal
many feelings and emotions, from pleasure and
welcome to hunger and fear. But as you will discover,
one animal is different from most others.
The panda can make a variety of noises
when it is excited or fearful, but for months at a
time it may make no noise at all. I was amazed to
learn from a zookeeper at the London Zoo
that he had not heard the pandas
make a noise in several years.

—F. S.

But What Does the Hippopotamus Say?

WRITTEN BY
Francesca Simon

ILLUSTRATED BY
Helen Floate

GULLIVER BOOKS
HARCOURT BRACE & COMPANY
San Diego   New York   London

For Sue Coughlin and Mark Gilbert
—with love and thanks

First published in 1994 by Pan Macmillan Children's Books, London

Text copyright © 1994 by Francesca Simon
Illustrations copyright © 1994 by Helen Floate

First U.S. edition 1994

Library of Congress Cataloging-in-Publication Data
available upon request.
ISBN 0-15-200029-1

Printed in Singapore

A B C D E

We all know that pigs OINK,

cats MEEEOW,

and horses NEIGH.
But what does the hippopotamus say?

HUNNNN

Cows MOO, ducks QUACK.
What about the long-haired yak?

GRR GRR GRR

Goats say MAA, sheep bleat BAA,

geese HONK and ravens CAW,
owls cry TU-WHIT TU-WHOO.

What about the kangaroo?

TSK TSK TSK

Chickens CHOOK CHOOK, pigeons COO.
What about the caribou?

ORRRRR

Snakes HISS, bees BUZZ,

turkeys GOBBLE GOBBLE GOBBLE.
Bears GROWL,

hyenas laugh.
What about the tall giraffe?

PWWWWW

Donkeys bray HEE-HAW HEE-HAW,

lions and tigers roar RAA,

the gray wolf howls AHWOO AHWOO.
What does the panda do?

Pandas don't

hum HUNNNN

or click TSK TSK TSK

or grunt GRR GRR GRR

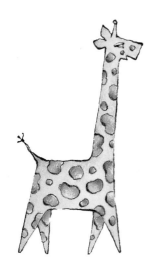

or blow PWWWWW

or call ORRRRR.

Pandas say. . .

. . . almost nothing at all!